19. Identify and use different kinds of verbs ar
20. Identify and use participles.
21. Change adjectives to adverbs by using the
22. Identify information and details by scannir
    slowly.
23. Identify graphic aids and their uses.
24. Summarize.
25. Compare and contrast characters.
26. Use reading skills in Bible study.
27. Identify four kinds of sentences and punctuate them correctly.
28. Identify complete sentences, subject and predicate parts.
29. Arrange words in correct order.
30. Improve sentences by adding adjectives, adverbs, and using words
    correctly.
31. Write dialogue.
32. Spell words correctly.

VOCABULARY

Review these words. Learning the meanings of these words is a good study habit and will improve your understanding of this LIFEPAC.

ballad (bal' ud). A poem or song that tells a story.

cadence (kā' duns). Rhythm.

comprehension (kom pri hen' shun). The act or power of understanding.

conundrum (ku nun' drum). A riddle whose answer involves a pun or play on words.

couplet (kup' lit). Two lines of poetry that belong together. They usually rhyme.

diacritical mark (dī u krit' u kul märk). A mark placed over a letter to show stress or
    accent.

dialogue (dī' u lôg). Conversation.

graphic (graf' ik). Of or about a drawing or picture.

heteronym (het' er ō nim). A word spelled like another word but different in
    pronunciation and meaning.

homonym (hom' u nim). A word having the same pronunciation as another word but
    a different meaning.

idiom (id' ē um). A phrase or expression whose meaning cannot be understood from
    the ordinary meanings of words.

infer (in fer'). To find out by thinking; to conclude.

3

inspirational (in' spu ra' shu nul). Filling a person with thought, feeling, excitement; influencing someone.

irregular (i reg' yu lur). Not according to rule; out of the usual order or natural way.

judgment (juj' munt). Decision; opinion.

limerick (lim' ur ik). A form of humorous nonsense verse with five lines and a certain rhyme pattern.

literary (lit' u rer ē). Having to do with literature.

metaphor (met' u fôr). A phrase or word that means one thing ordinarily but is applied to something else to make a comparison; a figure of speech.

negative (neg' u tiv). Not positive; saying no.

palindrome (pal' in drōm). Word, verse, or sentence that reads the same backward or forward.

personification (pur son' u fu kā' shun). A figure of speech in which a lifeless thing or quality is spoken of as if it is alive.

pun (pun). A humorous use of a word that can have two meanings.

quatrain (kwot' rān). Stanza or poem of four lines.

simile (sim' u lē). An expressed comparison of two different things or ideas using "like" or "as"; a likeness between things.

speculate (spek' yu lāt). Reflect; consider.

stanza (stan' zu). A group of lines of poetry, arranged according to a fixed plan.

stress (stres). Treat as important; put pressure on; emphasize.

summarize (sum' u rīz). To give only the main points.

symbolism (sim' bu liz um). Representation by symbols; use of symbols.

Note: All vocabulary words in this LIFEPAC appear in **boldface** print the first time they are used. If you are unsure of the meaning when you are reading, study the definitions given.

Pronunciation Key: hat, āge, cāre, fär; let, ēqual, tėrm; it, īce; hot, ōpen, ôrder; oil; out; cup, půt, rüle; child; long; thin; /TH/ for then; /zh/ for measure; /u/ represents /a/ in about, /e/ in taken, /i/ in pencil, /o/ in lemon, and /u/ in circus.

LANGUAGE ARTS 510

CONTENTS

Author: **Sandra Stone, M.A.**
Editor-in-Chief: Richard W. Wheeler, M.A.Ed.
Editor: Elizabeth Loeks Bouman
Consulting Editor: Rudolph Moore, Ph.D.
Revision Editor: Alan Christopherson, M.S.

Alpha Omega Publications ®

300 North McKemy Avenue, Chandler, Arizona 85226-2618
© MCMXCVI by Alpha Omega Publications, Inc.   All rights reserved.
LIFEPAC is a registered trademark of Alpha Omega Publications, Inc.

LANGUAGE ARTS 510

In this LIFEPAC® you will review Language Arts LIFEPACs 501 through 509. Reviewing all of this material is a big job! We do not want you to be overwhelmed like the boy in the illustration, so you will review only the basic concepts in literature, reading skills, grammar, and composition. For spelling, you will restudy twenty selected words from each LIFEPAC. You will also create your own folder of original compositions to share with your parents and friends. Follow the instructions below to prepare your folder. You will then be ready to add your compositions when indicated. Directions for what you will include in the folder will be given in two sections of this LIFEPAC.

Instructions for a Composition Folder

Materials needed: a 12" x 18" piece of construction paper, paper fasteners or yarn, writing paper (optional: poster paints, potato half)

Directions: Fold the construction paper in half. Choose a title and write it on the front of the folder along with your name (examples: "Notes by Ned," "Thoughts and Themes by Thelma," "Rachel's Writings," and so forth). Decorate your folder attractively. (Try this idea: Bring a potato half with a cut design from home. Dip the design in poster paint and print it on the folder.) Have your teacher check your folder.

 Teacher check _____

                         Initial   Date

OBJECTIVES

Read these objectives. The objectives tell you what you should be able to do when you have successfully completed this LIFEPAC.

When you have finished this LIFEPAC, you should be able to:

1. Identify six questions for judging a story's literary value.
2. Judge a story's value for character building by identifying good and bad character traits.
3. Identify three elements that make a story a pleasure to read.
4. Identify types of literature.
5. Identify forms of poetry.
6. Identify cadence, rhythm, rhyme, and stanzas.
7. Identify poetic devices.
8. Identify and use different kinds of nouns and pronouns.
9. Recognize the position and purpose of adjectives and use them correctly.
10. Identify an author's purpose and authority.
11. Identify the main idea, plot, setting, and characters.
12. Answer comprehension questions.
13. Infer or speculate about events.
14. Identify cause and effect.
15. Make Christian judgments.
16. Distinguish between fact and opinion.
17. Recognize the meanings of idioms.
18. Identify and use heteronyms.

I. SECTION ONE

In this section you will review literature, nouns and adjectives, as well as write some poetry and a short story, which will be included in your composition folder. You will review selected spelling words from Language Arts LIFEPACs 501, 502, and 503. In handwriting, you will review five handwriting tips.

SECTION OBJECTIVES

Review these objectives. When you have finished this section, you should be able to:

1. Identify six questions for judging a story's literary value.
2. Judge a story's value for character building by identifying good and bad character traits.
3. Identify three elements that make a story a pleasure to read.
4. Identify types of literature.
5. Identify forms of poetry.
6. Identify cadence, rhythm, rhyme, and stanzas.
7. Identify poetic devices.
8. Identify and use different kinds of nouns and pronouns.
9. Recognize the position and purpose of adjectives and use them correctly.
32. Spell words correctly.

Restudy these vocabulary words.

ballad	literary	quatrain
cadence	metaphor	simile
conundrum	palindrome	stanza
couplet	personification	stress
inspirational	pun	symbolism
limerick		

READING LITERATURE

Now you will review some information about literature, its definition, questions you should use to judge a story's **literary** value, character building, and the three elements that make a story a pleasure to read. Fiction, nonfiction, poetry, and Bible literary forms will also be reviewed.

Value of literature. In Language Arts LIFEPAC 509, literature was defined as *the body of writings of a period, language, or country, especially those writings kept alive by their beauty or effectiveness of style or thought.* You could not possibly read all the literature written in our language. You learned to decide whether a story is worth your time to read.

Review these questions you can ask yourself about the value of a story as literature from Language Arts LIFEPAC 505.

1. Is the story told in good, clear language?
2. Does the language match the kind of story told?
3. Does the language give you a feeling for the time of history in which the story takes place?
4. Is the language pleasant to read?
5. Does the language paint word pictures in your mind?
6. Do the characters seem to talk the way people of their age and time in history would?

 On the blanks, write the appropriate number or numbers of the preceding questions that best describe each selection.

1.1 _____ A long, long time ago, when Henry the Second was king of England, a youth was walking through Sherwood Forest.

1.2 _____ He was tall, strong, and comely. His woodland dress was a shirt and long green jerkin over long hose that covered his legs and hips. He wore soft leather boots on his feet and a blue hood on his head.

1.3 _____ As he strode through the greensward, he was hailed by a harsh voice. "Stand!" the voice cried. "Who art thou to march boldly through the king's greenwood?" (From "Robin Hood," LIFEPAC 504).

1.4 _____ He concentrated on his lunch until he heard something about government officials telling lies. His sandwich stuck in his throat. He tried to wash it down with his milk. The milk tasted funny. He looked up to see his mother eyeing him knowingly. (From "Roger Down and Roger Up," LIFEPAC 505).

You also learned to judge the value of a story for character building. As the story characters are developed, you learned to decide if the characteristics or qualities of these people are worthy to be admired. Do they have qualities of courage, unselfishness, or helpfulness? Are the characters mean, resentful, or greedy? Judging the characters by God's standards, do you want to be like them? Does the story help build good character in you?

Write *good* **or** *not good* **after each quotation or summary that shows the characters of people you have read about in previous LIFEPACs.**

1.5   "When Haman saw that Mordecai would not bow down or show reverence for him, he was furious. He planned a cruel scheme to rid the kingdom of not only Mordecai, but of every Jew." (Summary from "Esther," LIFEPAC 509) The character, Haman, is _____ .

1.6   "Queen Esther came before the king on behalf of her people despite the king's rule that no one should come before him unless called, or the person might be put to death." (Summary from "Esther," LIFEPAC 509) The character, Esther, is _____ .

1.7   "Cyrenius was a new believer, and even in his grief, he forgave my father." (Quotation from "Marc, LIFEPAC 507) The character, Cyrenius, is _____ .

1.8   "The Chief Forester began to beat the youngest of the woodsmen for showing his Saxon sullenness. . . . The forester rebuked the lad with a half dozen or more blows to his shoulder. . . ." (Quotation from "Robin Hood," LIFEPAC 504) The character, Chief Forester is

_____ .

Enjoying a story depends on three elements: kinds of words used, action of the story, and suspense. The kinds of words used will make the reader interested, move the action along, create a mood, and add suspense.

Match the item with the best description of each selection.

a. mood of sadness
b. action
c. suspense
d. mood of fear
e. mood of relief

1.9   _____   "Esther replied, 'Anyone who goes before the king without being called shall be put to death. . . . I will go to the king. If I die, then I die!' She put on her royal apparel and stood in the inner court of the palace. Would the king receive her?" (From "Esther," LIFEPAC 509)

1.10 _____   "As a child, he was teased by some older boys at the seashore. They wanted to throw him into the water to see if he could swim. At that time, he could not swim. Marc felt the boys moving in and his blood ran cold. A sick feeling hit the pit of his stomach. He wanted to run, but his feet were frozen to the ground." (From "Marc," LIFEPAC 507)

1.11 _____ "With a hard pull, I also loosened the strings that tied my hair down on the left side, but it hurt me terribly. . . Before I could seize them, the little people ran off shouting. . . instantly a hundred arrows struck my left hand like needles." (From "A Voyage to Lilliput," *Gulliver's Travels*, LIFEPAC 507)

1.12 _____ "He knew how he should make it right, and that's what was making his stomach sick and his heart pound. He went on, arguing with himself. 'If I tell her I lied, and I'm sorry, and I won't do it again, even if she punishes me, I'll feel better. I'll know I've done the right thing.'

By now he was running, and his heart was beginning to feel as light as his feet.

'If I hurry, I can do it before the afternoon classes start. I want to get it over with!" (From "Roger Down and Roger Up," LIFEPAC 505)

Types of literature. In Language Arts LIFEPACs 501 through 509, you studied many kinds of literature. Literature is usually classified as fiction or nonfiction. Fiction is writing that comes from the imagination. Nonfiction is writing that includes only what is fact. Short stories, novels, fables, legends, and drama are some types of fiction you have studied.

A fiction story that is short is called a *short story*. Short stories have only a few characters with brief descriptions. The characters live through something that happens during a few hours, a day, or a few days at most. The action is not too long or too involved. The short story is told from the author's or one of the character's point of view.

A *novel* is a longer story. It covers a longer period of time, like years, a lifetime or several generations. A novel uses long descriptions and shows how characters grow and why they make decisions. The story may be told from several points of view.

Fables are short stories that are meant to teach lessons. Most fables are about animals with some human characteristic, like talking. The lesson taught is called a moral. Aesop wrote many fables.

Legends are tales that were passed from generation to generation by word of mouth and are now continuing to be passed on through writing. Legends may have an element of historical truth, because the legendary person may have actually lived, but the events have become exaggerated through the years.

A *drama* is a story written to be acted in front of an audience in either a play or a movie. The time covered is usually short, but sometimes a drama covers two or three episodes widely separated by time. Stage or movie scene directions are given. The name of the person speaking is given in front of each spoken line.

Nonfiction is based completely on fact, or develops thoughts and opinions. History, biography (one person's life history), most newspaper writing, magazine article writing, and textbooks are nonfiction.

Many literary forms are found in the Bible. Short stories and history are found in both the Old Testament and New Testament. The Bible is filled with Hebrew poetry. Psalms are an excellent example of Hebrew poetry. Hebrew poetry does not rhyme. Proverbs are a form of Hebrew verse that uses the literary device of parallelism. Each proverb is written in two half sentences, closely tied together in thought. Parables are earthly stories that have heavenly meanings. Jesus told parables to teach people about God and heaven. A parable, like all good stories, has a setting, characters, plot, climax, and an ending. Parables use contrast. They contain truth or a spiritual meaning that is kept a secret from anyone who does not ask God to help him understand. Parables tell us what God expects from His children.

 Write *SS* (for short story), *N* (for novel), *P* (for parable), *D* (for drama), *F* (for fable), *L* (for legend), and *NF* (for nonfiction) on the line in front of the correct item.

1.13 _____ Tales passed from generation to generation.

1.14 _____ The action takes place within a few days time.

1.15 _____ Long descriptions are given.

1.16 _____ Contains a truth or spiritual meaning.

1.17 _____ Acted in front of an audience.

1.18 _____ The action covers a lifetime.

1.19 _____ A short story that is meant to teach a lesson or moral.

1.20 _____ Stage directions are given.

1.21 _____ Writing based completely on fact.

1.22 _____ It is an exaggerated tale.

1.23 _____ It has only a few characters with brief descriptions.

1.24 _____ History and newspaper writing are examples.

Write *true* **or** *false*.

1.25 _____ The Bible does not contain any short stories.
1.26 _____ Bible poetry rhymes.
1.27 _____ Parallelism is the literary device used in Proverbs.
1.28 _____ Fiction is writing that comes from the imagination.
1.29 _____ Parables have morals, and fables have spiritual meanings.

Poetry is another type of literature. You learned in Language Arts LIFEPAC 506 that poetry expresses strong feelings in a few words. The language and rhythm of poetry help create emotion. Every poem must have rhythm. The rhythm of a poem is found in a beat or **stress** that is heard when the poem is read aloud. Rhythm is made by stressed syllables. Listen for the stressed syllables in this example.

> **Example:** We're *shar*ing the *gar*den,
> As *friends* often *do.*

Another kind of rhythm is **cadence.** It is a rhythmical pattern that is not completely regular.

> **Example:** *De*licate *clo*ver and *feath*ery wild *car*rot *Cheer*fully *nod.*

Both kinds of rhythm have a kind of music you can hear if you try. Here is an example of a poem that rhymes. The rhyming words are in italics.

> **Example:** A tired caterpillar went to sleep one *day.* In a snug little cradle of silken *gray,*

You have also learned that poetry uses devices such as **metaphor**, **simile**, repetition of sounds, imitation of sounds, **personification**, and **symbolism**.

A *metaphor* compares two things. It calls one thing by another name in order to show it is like the other thing.

> **Example:** The pilot was an eagle soaring alone.

A *simile* is a phrase that compares one thing to another but uses the words *like* or *as.*

> **Example:** as hungry as a bear waking up in late winter

Repetition of sounds is a device that usually uses the beginning sound of words (like the *s* sound).

>   **Example:** A silly snake sadly sat

Imitation of sounds is a device that makes poetry lively.

>   **Example:** buzz of a bee

Personification is writing or speaking about a thing as if it were a person.

>   **Example:** The flowers reached up to the sun.

Symbolism is the use of one thing to stand for something else.

>   **Example:** A newborn babe is a symbol used in the Bible for a Christian.

Poems are written in **stanzas** rather than paragraphs.

 **Match by choosing the correct characteristic of poetry or poetic device for each item. Write the correct letter on each line. Use each letter only once.**

1.30 _____ The walls screamed with loneliness.

1.31 _____ He slept through the winter long and *cold,* All tightly up in his blanket *rolled.*

1.32 _____ The flight of the bird stood for the freedom now felt.

1.33 _____ The butterfly bid the blue bird good-bye.

1.34 _____ He was a bear of a man.

1.35 _____ When a poem has a beat made by stressed syllables.

1.36 _____ George roared like a lion.

1.37 _____ When a poem has a rhythmical pattern that is not completely regular.

1.38 _____ The bong of a bell rang softly.

1.39 _____ The form in which a poem is written.

a. rhythm

b. rhyme

c. cadence

d. metaphor

e. simile

f. repetition of sounds

g. personification

h. symbolism

i. imitation of sounds

j. stanza

A Child's Thought
by Carol Findlay[1]

If Jesus came to our house
   And knocked upon the door,
I'd ask Him in politely,
   And a glass of milk I'd pour.

I'd show Him where our rooms are,
   And where I always sleep;
I'd show Him all our bogie-holes,*   *places to
   And all the things I keep.   be afraid of

If Jesus came to our house
   And knocked upon the door,
I know I'd be more happy
   Than I ever was before.

You have studied different kinds of poetry in Language Arts LIFEPACs 502 and 506. You have read a story poem, a **ballad**, humorous poems, and **inspirational** poems. You read and learned to write poetry that plays with words: diamond poetry, **palindromes**, **conundrums**, **puns**, and **limericks**.

When storytellers tell stories in rhyme and rhythm, they tell story poems. Story poems that can be sung are called *ballads*. Story poems and ballads are usually in four-line stanzas. The ballad, "King John and the Abbot of Canterbury" (LIFEPAC 506), is an example of a humorous poem. Inspirational poems help us feel like being better people. Inspirational poems can inspire patriotism, love for God, Christlike characteristics, and other noble feelings.

Palindromes are words; phrases, or sentences that read the same backward as they read forward. *Conundrums* are riddles that play on words. *Puns* are also a play on words. To make a pun, you use a word that sounds like, or almost like, another word, or you use a word that has two meanings. *Limericks* usually start with a line like, "There once was a lady (or an old man) . . . ." *Diamond poetry* is shaped like a diamond. It has seven lines, beginning with a noun on the first line. Two adjectives describing the noun are on the second line; three participles describing the noun are on the third line; four more nouns are on the fourth line; three more participles are on the fifth line; and two adjectives are on the sixth line. Diamond poetry ends with a noun on the seventh line. The first and last nouns refer to the same person, animal, or thing. The mood changes in the middle of the poem.

[1]Reprinted from *Clear Shining After Rain* by E Margaret Clarkson (1962); William B. Eerdmans Co. Used by permission.

Match the correct type of poetry for each example or description. Write the correct letter on each line.

1.40 _____
                    lion
              angry, hungry
         stalking, hunting, running
tiredness, loneliness, leanness, strength,
        walking, panting, searching
           restless, fearsome
              hunter

a. story poem

b. ballad

c. inspirational poem

1.41 _____ Anna, Otto

1.42 _____ Stories told in rhyme and rhythm   d. diamond poetry

1.43 _____ There once was man from New York
Who loved to eat ham, beef, and pork.
Even after a feast   e. palindromes
His hunger increased,
So he ate his knife, spoon, and fork.   f. conundrum
           —William M. Stone

1.44 _____ What has only one horn and gives milk?   g. pun
           A milk truck.

1.45 _____ A story poem that can be sung   h. limerick

1.46 _____ The mountain told the little hill that it
would never amount to anything.

1.47 _____ I pray to God at break of day,
"Keep me walking in your way."
And as I close my eyes at night,
"Forgive my wrongs and make them right."

        In Language Arts LIFEPAC 506, you also studied four more poetic forms: pen picture, rhymed **couplet**, rhymed **quatrain**, and free verse. The pen picture is very short, only one stanza of three lines. Each line is a metaphor that describes the thing named by the title. The rhymed couplet is two lines with the same beat and rhymed end words. A rhymed quatrain is four lines of poetry that have a rhyming pattern. The possible rhyming patterns can be shown by assigning letters to the lines (examples: aabb, abab, abcb). Free verse has cadence, but it does not have a strict rhythm pattern, a rhyme pattern, a stanza pattern, or any certain length. The Bible has many examples of free verse.

Match by choosing the correct poetic form for each example. Write the correct letter on each line.

1.48 _____ A tired caterpillar went to sleep
      one day
In a snug little cradle of silken gray,
And he said, as he softly curled up
      in his nest,
"Oh, crawling was pleasant, but
      rest is best."
             —Author unknown

1.49 _____   A Fall Leaf
Red jam on baked bread;
A playful butterfly;
A crisp letter from winter's stationery.
            —Sandra J. Stone

1.50 _____ Our Father which art in heaven,
Hallowed be thy name.
Thy kingdom come.
Thy will be done,
on earth as it is in heaven.
          (Luke 11:2)

1.51 _____ I know that Christ has died for me.
He conquered sin and set me free.

a. pen picture

b. rhymed couplet

c. rhymed quatrain

d. free verse

USING NOUNS AND ADJECTIVES

As you review your study of nouns and adjectives, you will also solve a mystery.

King Milford received a note from his favorite squire. Alas! The note was torn. However, clues to the squire's whereabouts are circled and numbered in this section. Find the six clues and trace the path to the place the squire is being held captive.

Nouns. In Language Arts LIFEPAC 507 you studied common and proper nouns, singular and plural nouns, possessive nouns, nouns as subjects, nouns as objects of verbs, pronouns as noun substitutes, and possessive pronouns.

Common nouns are general names for a person, place, or thing. *Proper nouns* are specific (particular) names of certain people, places, or things. We show proper nouns by capitalizing the first letter.

Complete this activity.

1.52   Underline the common nouns in this list.

Rocky Mountains	drown	hurry
policeman	bakery	sword
joyful	tired	newspaper
California	bottle	climber

Complete these sentences with a common noun.

1.53   Jeff's father works in a _____ .
1.54   Karin saw a _____ in the forest.
1.55   She dropped a _____ on the floor.
1.56   John traded a _____ for a rare stamp.
1.57   He asked the _____ to fix his radiator.

 **Complete these sentences with proper nouns from this list.**

Baker Road	bridge	avenue
country	France	Pacific Ocean
river	Mrs. Thomas	First Bible Church

1.58   Becky studied in _____ this summer.

1.59   I swam in the _____ for the first time this year.

1.60   My house is on _____ .

1.61   _____ is Peggy's teacher.

1.62   Tom attends _____ every Sunday.

Common nouns may be in the singular or plural form. Singular form is used when the noun names only one person, place, or thing (girl, store). Plural form is used with more than one person, place, or thing (girls, stores). Changing a singular noun to a plural noun can be as simple as just adding *s*.

Some singular words, however, become plural by changing spelling. Review the five rules for changing singular nouns to plural nouns in Language Arts LIFEPAC 507.

 Read each word. Write *S* if it is singular. Write *P* if it is plural.

1.63   _____ citizens

1.64   ⟨____1____⟩ children

1.65   _____ roof

1.66   _____ ladies

1.67   ⟨____2____⟩ garage

 Change these singular nouns to their plural forms.

1.68   baby   _____

1.69   goose   _____

1.70   monkey   _____

1.71   fish   ⟨____3____⟩

1.72   branch   _____

16

Possessive nouns show ownership. Review these three rules for changing nouns to possessive nouns.

1. If the noun is singular, always add *'s*.
   Example: elephant   elephant's trunk

2. If the noun is plural already and ends in s, just add an apostrophe (').
   Example: two boys   two boys' car

3. If a plural noun does not end in s, then add *'s*.
   Example: the children   the children's toys

 Write the possessive noun of these singular and plural nouns.

1.73   men   _____

1.74   oxen   _____

1.75   kittens   _____

1.76   train   _____

1.77   traders   _____

1.78   lion   _____

Nouns may be used as subjects in noun phrases or as objects in verb phrases. Read the sentences below. They are divided into two parts—the subject (or noun phrase) and the predicate (or verb phrase). The nouns are in italics.

Noun phrase (subject)   **Verb phrase (predicate)**

The old *man*   sat on a *stool.*
The big *dog*   stared at the *food.*

 **Read these sentences.** Underline the noun in the noun phrase and circle the noun in the verb phrase.

1.79   The roaring river / flooded the valley.

1.80   The young girl / found a lost puppy.

1.81   The fireman / climbed the ladder.

1.82   The pianist / found her music.

1.83   The class / went to the library.

A *pronoun* is a noun substitute, because it is used in place of a noun.

Substitute a pronoun for the noun or noun phrase in italics in each sentence.

1.84   *Joe* visited his grandmother. ⟨_____ 4 _____⟩

1.85   *John, Jason, and Jeff* went to the park. _____

1.86   *Susan* is shopping for a new dress. ⟨_____ 5 _____⟩

1.87   *Sarah and I* are going to Jan's party. _____

Possessive pronouns take the place of possessive nouns. Possessive pronouns include *my, mine, his, her, its, their, our,* and *your.*

Substitute a possessive pronoun for the possessive noun in italics.

1.88   The fox ran into the *fox's* den. ⟨_____ 6 _____⟩

1.89   Janice could not find *Janice's* book. _____

1.90   The teacher displayed the *children's* art work. _____

Adjectives. Adjectives tell *what kind, how many,* and *which one.* Adjectives describe nouns. Remember, *the, a,* and *an* are adjectives.

Complete this activity.

1.91   Underline the adjectives.

table	pen	happy	sad
cabinet	green	soft	tall
loud	giraffe	many	raging

Adjectives are often found in front of nouns, describing them.

    Example: *The tiny, brown* mouse ran under *the old, yellow table.*

Adjectives may also be found after nouns.

    Example: *The* building is *tall.*

The word *tall* describes the building, even though it is not in front of it.

 **Underline the adjectives in these sentences.**

1.92   The busy beaver built a sturdy dam.
1.93   The dog is hungry.
1.94   The dark room was scary.
1.95   A small tree was planted by the winding stream.
1.96   The rose is beautiful.

Adjectives expand sentences and make them more interesting and exciting. Adjectives can express mood. They can even change the meaning of a sentence.

 Expand these sentences by adding adjectives to each noun.

1.97   A giant met a mouse.
_____

1.98   The boy was lost in the desert.
_____

1.99   The wolf hid in a cave.

_____

Now that you've reviewed nouns and adjectives, be sure you've helped King Milford get to the right place.

 **WRITING A SHORT STORY AND POETRY**

In this section, you will prepare your first selections for your composition folder. You will write a short story and two poems.

Short story. In Language Arts LIFEPAC 505 you learned how to collect "seed" ideas for writing a short story. Sources for seed ideas are news items, the newspaper, your own experiences, family history, team games, pictures, or anything you can imagine.

From your seed idea you develop a plot. You decide on the setting, characters, and the action. Remember that a short story has only a few characters with brief descriptions. The characters live through something that happens during a few hours, a day, or a few days at most. The action is not too long or too involved. The story should be told from your point of view or one of the character's points of view.

Read this example of an outline for a short story.

  I.   Setting - a cave
  II.   Characters - two boys, Jerry and Tom
  III. Action - Jerry and Tom lose their way in a cave. Tom sprains his ankle. Jerry continues to search for the opening and finally finds one. Jerry returns with help for Tom.

Fill in this guide for writing your short story.

1.100   I.   Setting _____

_____

II.   Characters _____

_____

III.   Action _____

_____

Review Language Arts LIFEPAC 505 for how to make your story grow and write your first draft. Then, write a rough draft of your story. Correct it for spelling, punctuation, grammar, and clear ideas.

Complete this activity.

1.101   On a separate piece of paper, copy your short story in your best handwriting. Place it in the composition folder you made at the beginning of this LIFEPAC.

Teacher check _____
                            Initial   Date

Poetry. Review the types of poetry mentioned earlier in this LIFEPAC. Choose two of the following types of poetry that you would like to write for your folder: diamond poetry, pen picture, rhymed quatrain, free verse, or limerick.

Complete this activity.

1.102   On separate pieces of paper, write two poems of your choice. Place each poem in your composition folder.

Teacher check _____
                            Initial   Date

SPELLING AND HANDWRITING
In this section, you will review twenty words from each of Language Arts LIFEPAC 501, 502, and 503. You will also review the five handwriting hints and practice spacing when you write.

Spelling. In Language Arts LIFEPAC 501, you learned to spell words that have a vowel diphthong, a vowel digraph, or a silent -*e*.

A vowel *diphthong* is a *blending of two speech sounds,* spelled with two vowel letters.

> **Examples:** -*oi* and -*oy* as in *oil* and t*oy*
> -*ou* and -*ow* as in *ouch* and c*ow*

A vowel *digraph* is *two vowels written together that make one sound.*

> **Examples:** -*ea* as in *eat*; -*ee* as in b*eet*; -*ay* as in s*ay*; -*oo* as in l*oo*k; -*ai* as in r*ai*n; and -*au* as in t*au*ght

The silent -*e* is found at the end of each word. Restudy the words in Review Words 501.

Spelling Words-1

Review Words 501

Vowel Diphthongs

abound	mountain	tower
boiling	poison	voyage
coward	royal	

Vowel Digraphs

booklet	creature	freedom
caution	failure	praying

Silent -*e*

arrange	mistake	suppose
college	secure	treasure

Complete these activities.

1.103   Fill in the charts. Use the review spelling words from Language Arts
LIFEPAC 501.

		Write the Vowel Diphthong	Write the First Syllable	Write the Second Syllable	Write the Word
a.	mountain	ou	moun	tain	
b.	abound				
c.	coward				
d.	tower				
e.	boiling				
f.	poison				
g.	royal				
h.	voyage				
		Write the Vowel Digraph	Write the First Syllable	Write the Second Syllable	Write the Word
i.	creature				
j.	caution				
k.	freedom				
l.	praying				
m.	booklet				
n.	failure				

1.104   Write six review words ending with a silent -*e*.

a. _____   c. _____   e. _____

b. _____   d. _____   f. _____

   You studied compound words, sight words, and contractions in
Language Arts LIFEPAC 502. A compound word is a word formed by
two words, two words separated by a hyphen, or two separate words
that go together for one meaning.

Sight words are words that are not spelled the way they sound. They can be tricky!

Contractions are two words joined together by dropping one syllable and adding an apostrophe. Restudy the words in Review Words 502.

Spelling Words-1

Review Words 502

Compound Words

afternoon	hardship	landscape
brand-new	inlet	moonlight
childhood		

Sight Words

believe	busy	raise
business	doctor	separate

Contractions

haven't	we'd	you're
she'll	won't	you've
should've		

Complete these activities.

1.105   Complete these compound words.

a. after _____   c. _____-new   e. ____hood   g. _____light

b. hard_____   d. in_____   f. land____

1.106   Write in the correct letters to complete these sight words.

a. bel__ __ve   c. doct__ __   e. rai__e

b. bu__y   d. bu__ine__ __   f. sep__ __ate

1.107   Write the contractions for these words.

a. have not   _____

b. will not   _____

c. she will   _____

d. you are   _____

e. we would   _____

f. should have   _____

g. you have   _____

23

In Language Arts 503 you learned to spell more words with vowel digraphs, words with silent letters, and antonyms.

Antonyms are pairs of words that have opposite meanings. Restudy the words in Review Words 503.

Spelling Words-1

Review Words 503

Vowel Digraphs

| automatic | betrayal | leadership |
| available | exceedingly | underneath |

Silent Letters

| chalk | glisten | sigh |
| flight | kneel | wrestle |

Antonyms

| advance-retreat | discourage-encourage |
| deny-admit | fact-fiction |

 **Complete these activities.**

1.108   Supply the missing digraphs for each of these words.

a.___ ___tomatic   c. av___ ___lable   e. undern___ ___th

b. betr___ ___al   d. l___ ___dership   f. exc___ ___dingly

1.109   Write the words with silent letters. Circle the silent letter or letters in each word.

a. _____   c. _____   e. _____

b. _____   d. _____   f. _____

1.110   Write the antonym for each of these words.

a. fiction   _____

b. admit   _____

c. discourage   _____

d. retreat   _____

 **Ask your teacher to give you a practice spelling test of Spelling Words-1.** Restudy any words you miss.

Handwriting. Review the five handwriting tips. You will practice spacing in this section. The remaining four tips will be practiced later in this LIFEPAC.

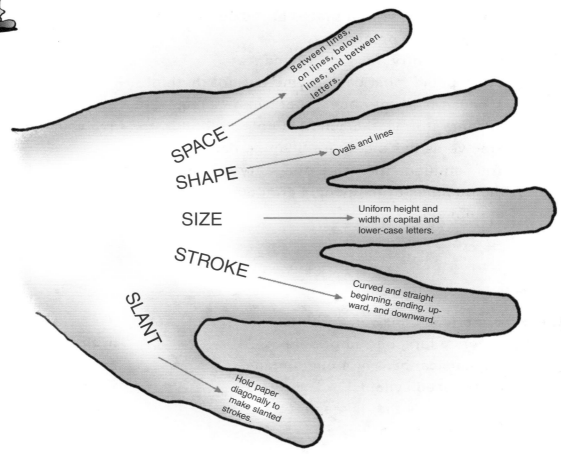

SPACE — Between lines, on lines, below lines, and between letters.

SHAPE — Ovals and lines

SIZE — Uniform height and width of capital and lower-case letters.

STROKE — Curved and straight beginning, ending, upward, and downward.

SLANT — Hold paper diagonally to make slanted strokes.

Rewrite this sentence, correctly using the proper spacing between letters and words.

1.111

Spacing is an important skill.

Review the material in this section to prepare for the Self Test. The Self Test will check your understanding of this section. Any items you miss on this test will show you what areas you need to restudy.

SELF TEST 1

Write *true* **or** *false* (each answer, 2 points).

1.01 _____ Fiction writing comes from the imagination.

1.02 _____ A legend is an example of nonfiction writing.

1.03 _____ Fables have spiritual meanings and parables have morals.

1.04 _____ Nonfiction is writing that is based completely on fact and develops thoughts and opinions.

1.05 _____ Hebrew poetry does not rhyme.

1.06 _____ Every poem must have rhyme but not rhythm.

1.07 _____ A ballad is a story poem that can be sung.

1.08 _____ In short stories, the action is not too long or too involved.

1.09 _____ Free verse has a definite rhyming pattern.

1.010 _____ You can judge the value of a story for character building by deciding if the qualities of the people are good or bad and if good moral values are upheld.

Match these items (each answer, 2 points).

1.011 _____ covers a long period of time

1.012 _____ the musical beat of a poem made by stressed syllables

1.013 _____ a short story that is meant to teach a lesson or moral

1.014 _____ a story written to be acted in front of an audience

1.015 _____ writing or speaking about a thing as if it were a person

1.016 _____ a phrase that compares one thing to another using the words *like* or *as*

1.017 _____ when one thing stands for something else

1.018 _____ an earthly story with heavenly meanings

1.019 _____ the form in which a poem is written

1.020 _____ an exaggerated tale

a. drama

b. novel

c. fable

d. legend

e. parable

f. rhythm

g. stanza

h. personification

i. symbolism

j. simile

k. metaphor

Choose the correct answer for each item by writing the letter and the answer on the line (each answer, 2 points).

1.021   The reader's enjoyment of a story depends on three elements: kinds of words, action of the story, and _____ .
      a. metaphors   b. suspense   c. length of story

1.022   Short stories have _____ .
      a. only a few characters
      b. long descriptions
      c. many characters

1.023   A type of fiction that uses long descriptions and shows how characters grow and why they make decisions is the _____ .
      a. short story   b. legend   c. novel

1.024   A type of Bible literature that contains a spiritual meaning that is kept a secret from anyone who does not ask God to help him understand is
_____ .
      a. a parable   b. a fable   c. poetry

1.025   A rhythmical pattern that is not completely regular is _____ .
      a. syllables   b. cadence   c. imitation of sounds

1.026   "Clang, clang, clang went the bell," is an example of _____ .
      a. imitation of sounds   b. symbolism   c. cadence

1.027   "The big bear broke the branch," is an example of _____ .
      a. personification   b. a simile   c. repetition of sounds

1.028   Pen picture, rhymed couplet, and rhymed quatrain are examples of
_____ .
      a. stanzas   b. free verse   c. poetic form

1.029   Poems that help us feel like being a better person are called
_____ .
      a. inspirational poems   b. palindromes   c. diamond poetry

1.030   A poem which usually starts with a line like, "There was an old lady (or an old man) from . . . ." is called a _____ .
      a. pun   b. limerick   c. conundrum

Complete these sentences with a common noun or a proper noun from the list. Write *PN* or *CN* over the noun (each numbered answer, 4 points).

      hospital   England   mountain   professor   Mr. Jones

1.031   I was born in _____ .

1.032   The _____ left school yesterday.

Change each singular noun to its plural form (each answer, 2 points).

1.033   paper   _____

1.034   lady   _____

1.035   child   _____

Change each singular or plural noun to its possessive form (each answer, 2 points).

1.036   pastors   _____

1.037   aunt   _____

1.038   sheep   _____

Underline the noun that is the subject of each sentence. Circle the noun that is the object of the verb in each sentence (each correct word, 2 points).

1.039   The young man / wrote a story.

1.040   The shepherds / grazed their sheep.

Substitute a pronoun for the underlined noun(s) (each answer, 1 point).

1.041   The teacher sent <u>Susan</u> and <u>Ann</u> home. _____

1.042   <u>Gary</u> lost his lunch. _____

Write a possessive pronoun in each blank (each answer, 2 points).

1.043   The turtle turned over on _____ back.

1.044   Sarah turned _____ paper in late.

Expand this sentence by adding adjectives with each noun (this answer, 3 points).

1.045   The sun came up over the mountains.

_____

_____

Answer this question (this answer, 5 points).

1.046   What are three of the six questions you can ask yourself about the value of a story as literature?

_____

_____

_____

_____

_____

_____

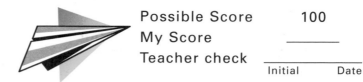

Take a spelling test of Spelling Words-1.

II. SECTION TWO

In this section you will review reading **comprehension** skills and word study skills. You will also review the use of verbs and adverbs. You will restudy selected spelling words from Language Arts LIFEPACs 504, 505, and 506. In handwriting, you will practice two more handwriting tips.

SECTION OBJECTIVES

Review these objectives. When you have finished this section, you should be able to:

10. Identify an author's purpose and authority.
11. Identify the main idea, plot, setting, and characters.
12. Answer comprehension questions.
13. Infer or speculate about events.
14. Identify cause and effect.
15. Make Christian judgments.
16. Distinguish between fact and opinion.
17. Recognize the meanings of idioms.
18. Identify and use heteronyms.
19. Identify and use different kinds of verbs and adverbs.
20. Identify and use participles.
21. Change adjectives to adverbs by using the -*ly* suffix.
32. Spell words correctly.

Restudy these vocabulary words.

comprehension   idiom   judgment
diacritical mark   infer   negative
heteronym   irregular   speculate
homonym

USING READING COMPREHENSION SKILLS

You have studied many reading **comprehension** skills in previous LIFEPACs. These skills help you understand (comprehend) what you read. Now, review these reading comprehension skills.

Author's purpose and authority. Finding the author's purpose helps you understand and enjoy what you are reading. An author may want to entertain you, to inform you of something, to give you certain facts, to give you a set of directions, or to influence your thinking.

Also, consider the author's authority. Has the author given accurate and truthful information? Review these three questions you might ask to test an author's information.

1. Does the author have enough background experience to be authoritative about the subject?
2. Does the information given by the author agree with information about this topic?
3. Is the author's information consistent?

Read and answer each question.

Armstrong Sperry wrote the book, *Call it Courage,* a story of the brave adventures of a Polynesian folk hero called Mafatu. Mr. Sperry was a sailor who explored the South Pacific, and listened to his great grandfather tell of his adventures as a sea captain in the South Seas. ("The Flight," LIFEPAC 502)

2.1   What was Armstrong Sperry's purpose for writing *Call it Courage*?

_____

_____

2.2   Do you think Armstrong Sperry had the authority to write an adventure story about the South Seas? Why? _____

_____

_____

_____

_____

Main idea and plot, setting, and characters. The main idea is a summary of what was said in a certain paragraph or reading selection. The main idea of a paragraph can be given in one or two sentences.

An entire story can be summarized in a sentence. You had to identify the setting, characters, and plot (action) as a basic outline for the short story you wrote. Identifying these from reading material is also an important comprehension skill.

Read this summary from "The Farmer, His Son, and the Donkey" (LIFEPAC 508).

A farmer needed to sell his donkey. He decided no one should ride the donkey on the way to the market so that it would not be hot and tired when they arrived. Some girls laughed as the farmer and his son passed by with the donkey because they were not riding the donkey, so the father placed the son on the donkey's back. Then some elderly gentlemen chided the son for letting his poor father walk, so the father rode the donkey. Later, some women accused the man of cruelty to his son because his son was walking, so both rode the donkey to the market. As the three crossed the bridge to the market town, some farmers accused the farmer and his son of being cruel to the donkey by both riding him at the same time. The farmer and his son then picked up the donkey to carry him! At this, the donkey decided he had had enough, kicked himself free, and trotted home.

Complete these activities.

2.3 Choose the main idea. Put an *X* on the blank.
_____ Never carry a donkey.
_____ You cannot please everyone.
_____ Tell your donkey before you sell it.

2.4 Identify the setting, characters, and plot (action) of the summary of "The Farmer, His Son, and the Donkey."

    I.   Setting _____

            _____

    II.   Characters _____

            _____

    III.   Plot (action) _____

            _____

            _____

            _____

            _____

            _____

Sequence of events and comprehension questions. The events of any story always happen in a certain sequence, or order. Being able to place the events of a reading selection in their proper order is an important reading skill. The best way to do "sequence" activities is to read *all* the listed sentences first. Decide the first and last activities of the sequence and then work out the rest.

Comprehension questions are simply questions asked to see if you understood what you read.

Read this excerpt from "A Voyage to Lilliput" (LIFEPAC 507).

The emperor gently asked me to give up my knife. In the meantime, three thousand of his best troops surrounded me with bows and arrows. I drew out my knife from its holder and gently threw it on the ground. Next he demanded one of my hollow iron tubes, which was one of my pocket pistols. I drew it out, told him what it was used for, and then charged it with powder. First I warned the emperor not to be afraid, and then I shot it in the air. Hundreds fell down as if they were dead. Even the emperor was shocked. I gently delivered both my pistols and my bag of powder and bullets, warning him to keep them from fire or they would blow up his palace.

Complete these activities.

2.5 Number the events in the order they happened.
a. _____ I took it out, told him what it was used for, and charged it with powder.
b. _____ The emperor asked me to give up my knife.
c. _____ Three thousand soldiers surrounded me.
d. _____ The emperor asked for my pistol.
e. _____ I warned the emperor and then shot the pistol.
f. _____ I threw my knife on the ground.
g. _____ I gently delivered my pistols, powder, and bullets.
h. _____ The people fell down if as they were dead.

Answer this question.

2.6 Why did the troops surround Gulliver? _____

_____

_____

Inference and implied meaning. When you **infer** something, you draw a conclusion from information given to you. You **speculate** or conclude what happened. Readers sometimes have to infer what has taken place between two events because the writer does not specifically tell what happened. The reader uses his or her life experiences to draw an inference about the missing information.

To *imply* is to suggest a meaning only hinted at, without saying it outright. Many times, writers imply things by only giving the reader hints, not coming right out and saying it. This requires the reader to think about the reading and makes it more enjoyable.

Read this excerpt from "Esther" (LIFEPAC 509).

Queen Esther soon found out from Mordecai all the evil that Haman was planning. Mordecai pleaded with her to save her people. Esther replied to Mordecai, "Anyone who goes before the king without being called shall be put to death unless the king holds out the golden scepter, that he may live. I have not been called for thirty days."

Answer this question.

2.7 What do you think Esther meant when she replied, "Anyone who goes before the king without being called shall be put to death unless the king holds out the golden scepter, that he may live. I have not been called for thirty days?" _____

_____

_____

Read this item and answer the question.

In the story of "Esther," Esther went before the king. He was pleased to see her. King Ahasuerus told Esther, "Whatever you want or request, it shall be given you to the half of my kingdom." Not wanting to make her request then, Esther invited the king and Haman to a special banquet. At the banquet the king again made his offer to Esther.

2.8 What do you infer or speculate happened between the queen's invitation to the banquet and the banquet? _____

_____

Cause and effect. *Cause* is what makes something happen. The *effect* is the result, or the outcome.

Read the excerpt from "Abused Language in the Garden" (LIFEPAC 503).

Satan, the serpent, asked Eve the question, ". . . hath God said, Ye shall not eat of every tree of the garden?" (Genesis 3)

Eve replied (verse 2) "We may eat of the fruit of the trees of the garden: But of the fruit of the tree which is in the midst of the garden, God hath said, Ye shall not eat of it, . . . lest ye die."

The serpent then planted doubt about God's honesty in Eve's mind with these words (Genesis 3, 4, and 5), ". . . Ye shall not surely die: For God doth know that in the day ye eat thereof, then your eyes shall be opened, and ye shall be as gods, knowing good and evil." The serpent used that language to make it appear that God was not honest and was trying to keep Adam and Eve from becoming all they could be! Eve believed the serpent and looked at the fruit on the forbidden tree. It looked delicious, so she touched it, ate it, and shared it with Adam.

Answer these questions.

2.9   What caused Eve to eat and share the fruit with Adam? _____
_____

2.10   What was the effect of Eve's believing the serpent and disobeying God?
_____
_____

Christian judgments. When we make Christian **judgments**, we decide what is right and wrong according to God's Word.

Read each item. Make a judgment as to whether the action was right or wrong. Check the correct box.
Right   Wrong

2.11   ☐   ☐   ". . .Marc remembered another time when he was afraid. As a child, he was teased by some older boys at the seashore. They wanted to throw him into the water to see if he could swim." (From "Marc," LIFEPAC 507)
Was the action of the boys right or wrong?

2.12   ☐   ☐   "Marc's father stumbled and fell across the floor. Marc's mother reached down to help him up. Marc's mother was a gentle woman. She always helped those in need, whether it was a small, hurt animal or a friend in danger." (From "Marc," LIFEPAC 507)
Was the action of Marc's mother right or wrong?

	Right	**Wrong**	

2.13 □ □   "'I am Robert Fitzooth, though many call me Robin Hood. I am on my way to Nottingham to become one of the King's Foresters.' At this, the men laughed scornfully. They hurled all manner of insults at Robin." (From "A Tale of Long Ago," LIFEPAC 504)
Was the action of the men right or wrong?

2.14 □ □   "Dick went to work immediately helping the cook. . . She continually scolded him, "You never do anything." She worked him hard and was often mean to him. (From "Dick Whittington and His Cat," LIFEPAC 509)
   Was the action of the cook right or wrong?

Fact and opinion. A *fact* is a statement that can be proven. An *opinion* is a statement that tells what a person thinks or feels. Sometimes words like "probably," "think," or "believe" are used with opinions.

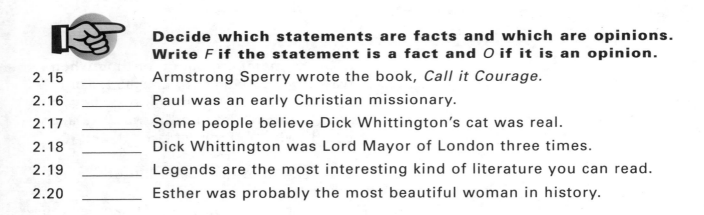

Decide which statements are facts and which are opinions. Write *F* if the statement is a fact and *O* if it is an opinion.

2.15 _____ Armstrong Sperry wrote the book, *Call it Courage.*

2.16 _____ Paul was an early Christian missionary.

2.17 _____ Some people believe Dick Whittington's cat was real.

2.18 _____ Dick Whittington was Lord Mayor of London three times.

2.19 _____ Legends are the most interesting kind of literature you can read.

2.20 _____ Esther was probably the most beautiful woman in history.

USING WORD STUDY SKILLS
   You have studied and will review word study skills making prefix and suffix words, compound words, and abbreviations in your spelling sections. You will now review other word study skills such as using **diacritical marks** and respellings, identifying **heteronyms**, and interpreting **idioms**.

LANGUAGE ARTS

ARTS 5 1 0

LIFEPAC TEST

80 / 100

Name _____

Date _____

Score _____

LANGUAGE ARTS 510: LIFEPAC TEST

Write *true* **or** *false* (each answer, 2 points)

1. _____ We should judge the value of a story on character building and especially ask if the characters are worthy to be admired.
2. _____ The reader's enjoyment of a story depends on the words used, action of the story, and suspense.
3. _____ Poetry in the Bible follows the rules of Hebrew poetry.
4. _____ Palindromes, conundrums, and puns are examples of poetry that plays on words.
5. _____ Cause is a result, or outcome.
6. _____ Comprehension questions are asked to see if you understand what you read.
7. _____ A main idea is usually several paragraphs in length.
8. _____ A reader scans material for its general content.
9. _____ A caption is a phrase that is not easily understood.
10. _____ You read *all* the material when you skim.

Match these items (each answer, 2 points).

11. _____ the beat heard when a poem is read aloud
12. _____ to entertain, inform, or influence thinking
13. _____ what a person "thinks" or "feels"
14. _____ writing that comes from the imagination
15. _____ decide what is right or wrong according to God's Word
16. _____ tell likenesses and differences
17. _____ body of writing of a period, language, or country
18. _____ a conversation
19. _____ tell main ideas or actions of a story as briefly as possible
20. _____ two lines of poetry with the same beat and rhymed end words

a. fiction
b. stress
c. rhymed couplet
d. literature
e. author's purpose
f. Christian judgment
g. ballad
h. opinion
i. compare and contrast
j. summarize
k. dialogue

Choose the correct answer. Write the letter and the answer on the line (each answer, 2 points).

21.   You should ask yourself questions like, "Was the story told in good clear language, and did the language paint word pictures?" when _____ .
         a. judging character
         b. judging a story's literary value
         c. reading a newspaper

22.   The two main classifications of literature are _____ .
         a. fiction and nonfiction
         b. fiction and history
         c. poetry and short stories

23.   The story of the "Lost Son" also has a spiritual meaning. It is an example of a _____ .
         a. short story   b. parable   c. poem

24.   Examples of poetic devices are metaphor, simile, personification, and _____ .
         a. conundrum   b. limerick   c. symbolism

25.   A summary of all that is said in a reading selection is called the _____ .
         a. sequence of events   b. main idea   c. literary value

26.   The term, "caught a cold," is an example of _____ .
         a. an idiom   b. a heteronym   c. implied meaning

27.   In the sentence, "Please *read* the book that I *read* yesterday," the word *read* is a(n) _____ .
         a. idiom   b. heteronym   c. homonym

28.   A drawing that shows size, how something is used, how it works or is put together is called a(n) _____ .
         a. chart   b. illustration   c. diagram

29.   To picture major historical events, you would use _____ .
         a. a time line   b. an illustration   c. a map

30.   The reading skill you did not use in your Bible study Psalm 37 was_____ .
         a. reading slowly for details
         b. charting information
         c. speculating about events

Rewrite this sentence in the proper order (this answer, 3 points).

31.　　The boy saw the dolphin in the car.

_____

Punctuate the dialogue correctly (this answer, 3 points).

32.　　___Will you be in school tomorrow ___ ___ asked the teacher ___ Jeff replied
　　　　___ ___No, I'm going on vacation ___ ___

Write CS if the item is a complete sentence and N if it is not a sentence (each answer, 2 points).

33.　_____　The tree was loaded with ripe pears.

34.　_____　Stuck to the glue.

Write the possessive form for each word (each answer, 2 points).

35.　truck　_____

36.　dogs　_____

Underline the subject part and circle the predicate part of this sentence (each answer, 2 points).

37.　　The leaves on the trees are changing color.

Write the word or words from each sentence that match its description (each answer, 2 points).

　　　　The falling snow covered the Rocky Mountains.

38.　participle used as an adjective modifier _____

39.　proper noun _____

40.　common noun _____

41.　verb _____

The black tornado is moving violently through the town.

42.　adjective _____

43.　helping verb _____

44.　adverb _____

45.　participle _____

The peacock never saw its majestically beautiful tail.

46.　negative adverb _____

47.　possessive pronoun _____

48.　adverb modifying an adjective _____

Take your LIFEPAC Spelling Test.

Diacritical marks and respellings. The dictionary helps you pronounce words correctly by using diacritical marks and respellings. Diacritical marks show how the vowels are pronounced. Respellings show how many syllables the word has and where the accent mark is placed in a word.

Study the respelling, diacritical marks, and meaning of each word.
Answer the questions.

(sil' u bul). A word or part of a word with one vowel sound.

2.21   What syllable is accented? _____
2.22   How many syllables are in the word? _____
2.23   What is the correct spelling of the word? _____

(u brē' vē ā' shun). The shortened form of a word.

2.24   How many long vowels are in the word? _____
2.25   How many syllables are in the word? _____
2.26   What is the correct spelling of the word? _____

Idioms. Idioms are phrases with meanings that cannot be understood from the ordinary meaning of the words in it. Authors use idioms to make their stories interesting and sometimes humorous.

Match the idiom with its meaning.

2.27   _____ in a jam   a. useless and strange
2.28   _____ lost in a book   b. in trouble
2.29   _____ uptight   c. decided not to do something
2.30   _____ got cold feet   d. avoid answering directly by talking
2.31   _____ stay cool   about something else
2.32   _____ beat around the bush   e. very interested in a book
2.33   _____ white elephant   f. very nervous about something
                                           g. remain calm

Complete this activity.

2.34   Choose two idioms from the preceding list. Write two sentences using each idiom.
        a. _____
        b. _____

Heteronyms. Certain words need to be identified by the way they are used in sentences. Read these sentences.

> **Example:** I will lead the way.
> The pencil lead broke.

The word *lead* has the same spelling, but a different meaning and pronunciation in each sentence.
Heteronyms are words that are spelled the same but have different meanings and are pronounced differently.

Complete this activity.

2.35 Study the heteronyms and the respellings that show how the words should be pronounced. Write a sentence for each respelling using the word correctly.

wind	a.	(wīnd)	_____
	b.	(wind)	_____
	c.	(ri kôrd')	_____
record	d.	(rek' urd)	_____
	e.	(rēd)	_____
read	f.	(red)	_____

USING VERBS AND ADVERBS

In Section I you helped King Milford find the place where his squire was being held captive. After thoroughly searching the Black Knight's castle, poor King Milford found another note.

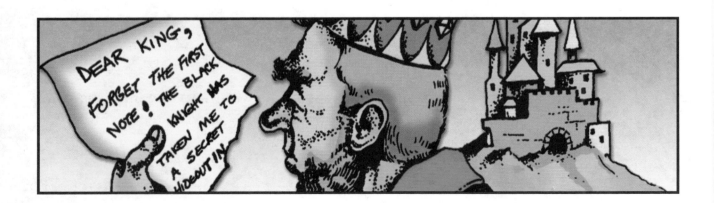

As you review verbs and adverbs, follow the clues to the secret hideout. You will find the clues circled and numbered in this section.

Verbs. In Language Arts 508 you studied verbs of being, verbs of action, singular, plural, past, present and future verb forms, regular and irregular verbs, and participles.

Verbs tell the reader what is happening, what has happened, or what is going to happen. A verb that expresses action is called an *action verb*. A verb that tells what the subject is, is called a *verb of being.*

Complete this activity.

2.36   Write the word *action* or *being* on the line after each verb.

a. work   _____   g. leap   _____

b. is   _____   h. am   _____

c. fishing   _____   i. were   _____

d. search   _____   j. eat   _____

e. was   (_____1_____)   k. shout   _____

f. are   _____   l. raced   _____

Complete each sentence with a verb of being or a verb of action.

2.37   Margaret _____ with the girl next door.

2.38   A koala _____ not a bear.

2.39   Jeff _____ on the wet sidewalk.

2.40   The children _____ hungry.

2.41   The lumberjack _____ the tree.

Certain forms of each verb tell you whether the action is happening at the present, happened sometime in the past, or will happen sometime in the future. Such a form expresses *verb tense*. Verb tense expresses the *time of an action*. You have studied three tenses of verbs: present, past, and future. Review the following chart.

Tense	The Time of Action	Example
Past tense	An action has happened.	The dog *chased* the cat.
Present tense	An action is happening.	The dog *is chasing* the cat.
Future tense	An action is going to happen.	The dog *will chase* the cat.

You have learned that verbs show past tense by changing form. The past tense forms are known as regular and **irregular**. Regular verbs form the past tense by adding the suffix *-ed (-d)* to the original word. Irregular verbs form the past tense by making changes within the word, so that the past tense looks like a new word. Review the two charts of regular and irregular verbs and their tenses. These charts show just a few examples.

Regular Verbs

Present tense	Past tense	Future tense
walk	walked	will walk
talk	talked	will talk
pray	prayed	will pray
share	shared	will share
drop	dropped	will drop

Irregular Verbs

Present tense	Past tense	Future tense
begin	began	will begin
break	broke	will break
come	came	will come
bring	brought	will bring
is	was	will be

 Underline the verb in each sentence. On the first line after each sentence write *past, present*, **or** *future* **to show the tense. On the second line write** *regular* **or** *irregular*.

		Tense	**Form**
2.42	Tom brought in the newspaper.	_____	_____
2.43	Janet cleaned her room.	_____	_____
2.44	Jesus will return again.	_____	_____
2.45	Daniel prayed three times a day.	⬭ 2	_____
2.46	The children share their toys.	_____	_____
2.47	The Larsens sold their home.	_____	_____
2.48	Jason is sick today.	_____	_____
2.49	We will pray for him.	_____	_____

Verbs and nouns must agree in number. Singular verbs must be used with singular subjects (nouns). Plural verbs must be used with plural subjects.

These examples illustrate the use of a singular verb with a singular subject.

The child *is* happy with his work.
The child *was* happy with his work.
The child *will* be happy with his work.

These examples illustrate how plural subjects and verbs agree.

These children *are happy* with their work.
These children *were happy* with their work.
These children *will be happy* with their work.

 Complete these sentences. Write the correct forms of the verbs *is, am, are, were,* and *was* so that the verbs and nouns agree in number.

2.50   I _____ not alone because God is with me.

2.51   The animals _____ lost in a storm.

2.52   The book (___3___) in the library.

2.53   The girls _____ at the park.

2.54   She _____ sorry for the mistake.

Certain verb forms are known as *participles*. Participles express action or being but they cannot serve as main verbs by themselves.

Present participles end in *-ing*. Past participles end in *-ed, -d, -t, -en, or -n*. A participle may be used as a main verb if a helping verb is used with it. The helping verb is a form of the verb *be*.

Example: She   *was*   *singing.*
                      (helping   (present
                      verb)   participle)

 Underline the complete verb (the helping verb and the participle) in each sentence.

2.55   The boys are studying in their room.
2.56   Margaret will be going to the concert.
2.57   Jan was bowling with a friend.
2.58   She is buying a new notebook.
2.59   The puppy was sold two days ago.

A participle may be used as an adjective modifier.
Examples: The *howling* wind woke the family.
The *broken* lamp was restored.

Complete this activity.

2.60   Underline the participles that are used as adjectives in this paragraph.

The raging storm swept the entire village. A scared girl found a hiding place. Her concerned mother searched everywhere. Pounding rain flooded the streets. Suddenly, the praying mother discovered a small human form in a large old box. With thanks to God, she gently carried her sleeping daughter home.

Adverbs. Adverbs usually modify or describe verbs, but they may also modify adjectives and other adverbs. They describe verbs by telling *how, when*, and *where*. The adverb may come before the verb or between a helping verb and a participle.

How	**When**	**Where**
talked *softly*	was *soon* coming	walked *everywhere*

Underline the adverb in each sentence.

2.61   The girl walked quietly into the room.

2.62   The parachute landed there.

2.63   He was cautiously driving home.

2.64   The soloist sang perfectly.

2.65   The lion ran quickly after its prey.

Adverbs may also modify or describe adjectives.

Example: Sam hit a perfectly pitched ball.
                          adv.   adj.

Underline the adverb and circle the adjective it modifies.

2.66   The young girl had an extremely radiant smile.
2.67   Jeff played a really great game.
2.68   The donkey was carrying a fairly heavy load.
2.69   She left a neatly organized desk.
2.70   The boy had a rapidly deteriorating condition.

Adverbs may also modify other adverbs.
  Example: Susan plays the piano *very* well.
                                    adv. adv.

Write an adverb from the list on the line in front of the adverb already in the sentence.

too   quite   very

2.71   He finished his work _____ rapidly.
2.72   She is driving _____ fast.
2.73   Paul entered the room _____ quietly.

Adjectives can become adverbs by changing the spelling of the word. Adverbs that modify verbs usually have the *-ly* suffix.

	adjective	**adverb**
Examples:	loving	lovingly
	happy	happily

Change the adjective at the end of the line into an adverb and write it on the line.

2.74   The horse ran _____ (swift).

2.75   The children yawned _____ (sleepy).

2.76   The star shone _____ (bright).

2.77   The sailor could see the island _____ (clear).

2.78   He wrote his name _____ (careless).

Fast, faster, and *fastest* are adverbs that show degrees of comparison. The chart will teach you the name of the degree of comparison and the suffix used to make a word show the degree of comparison.

Degree	What It Does	Suffix	Sample
Positive	simply modifies	none	fast
Comparative	compares two things	-er	faster
Superlative	compares three things	-est	fastest

Some adverbs, comparing two things, use *more* and *better*. Some adverbs, comparing three things, use *most* and *best*.

Complete the sentences using the positive, comparative, and superlative forms of these adverbs.

well   better   best

2.79   Jane reads _____ . (positive)

2.80   Sally reads _____ . (comparative)

2.81   Peggy reads ⟨_____⟩ . (superlative)
                                    5

Negative adverbs express negative meanings. The following words are negative adverbs.

hardly	scarcely	barely	nothing	none
never	no	only	but	nobody

Choose a negative adverb from the list to complete each sentence.

2.82   We have _____ used all our allotted supplies.
2.83   The dog _____ touched his dinner.
2.84   You can _____ blame them for being frightened.

Don't forget about King Milford. Did you help him find the right path?

SPELLING AND HANDWRITING

You will now review three more sets of twenty words each from Language Arts LIFEPACs 504, 505, and 506. In addition, you will review two handwriting tips: shape and size of letters.

Spelling. In Language Arts LIFEPAC 504 you learned to spell words with silent letters, words with variant sounds of *f* and *c*, and **homonyms**.

Silent letters can begin words, be found within the words, or be a silent partner in a double consonant. The /f/ sound in a word may be spelled with a *ph*, *gh*, or *f*. The soft *c* sounds like an *s*, and the hard *c* sounds like a *k*. Be careful! Homonyms are words that are pronounced the same but have different meanings and spellings.

Restudy the words in Review Words-504.

Spelling Words-2

Review Words 504

Silent Letters

| banner | ghost | listen |
| castle | knife | muscle |

Variants of *f* and *c*

celery	confident	cucumber
citizen	cough	fantastic
compliment		

Homonyms

| boarder | oar | pear |
| border | or | pair |

 **Complete these activities.**

2.85   Circle the silent letters in these words.
a. banner   c. listen   e. castle
b. knife   d. muscle   f. ghost

2.86   Complete each word with the correct letters to make the /f/ sound.
a. ___antastic   b. cou___ ___   c. ___ ___ysical

2.87   Write the words with a soft *c* (/s/) sound and a hard c (/k/) sound.

      Soft c   *Hard c*

   a. _____   c. _____   e. _____

   b. _____   d. _____   f. _____

2.88   Write the correct homonym on each line.

   a. The new _____ came from south of the _____ .

   b. Jack had to find the other _____ for the boat _____

     forget his trip on the lake.

   c. He lost a _____ of shoes under the _____ tree.

You learned to spell words with prefixes (*anti-, con-, pro-*) and suffixes (*-ment, -less, -ist, -ism, -th, -ish*) in Language Arts LIFEPAC 505. Restudy the words in Review Words 505.

Spelling Words-2

Review Words 505

amazement	employment	materialism
Americanism	enjoyment	program
antichrist	foolish	progress
antidote	fortieth	realism
confront	fourth	restless
context	helpless	scientist
eighth	heroism	

Solve the crossword puzzle.

2.89   Use Review Words 505.

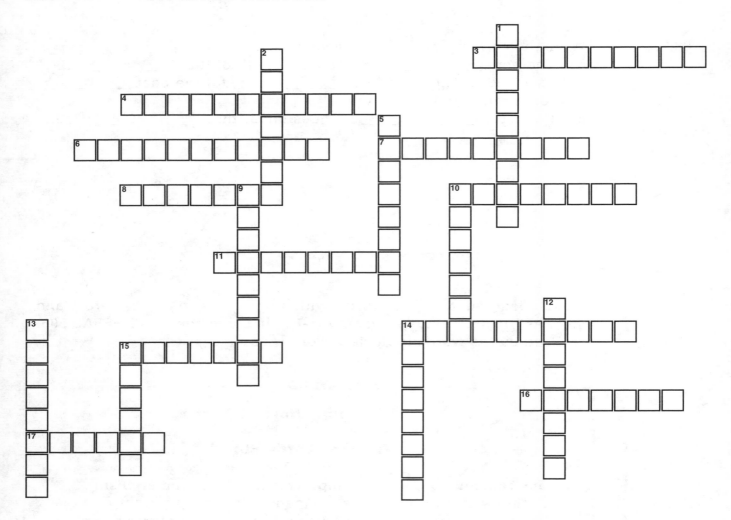

Across

3. work
4. a tendency to care too much for material things
6. devotion to the United States
7. pleasure
8. great courage
10. meet face to face
11. without help
14. the great enemy or opponent of Christ
15. without sense
16. list of items or events
17. next after seventh

Down

1. great surprise
2. thoughts and actions based on realities alone
5. uneasy
9. person who knows much about science
10. words directly before or after a word or sentence that influence its meaning
12. moving forward
13. next after thirty-ninth
14. a remedy
15. next after third

48

In Language Arts LIFEPAC 506, you learned to spell more words with suffixes *(-tion, -ward, -ious, -ous, -ship, -some)* and also irregular plurals. Some of the suffix words are easy to make because you just add the suffix to the root word. For others you have to remember to drop the *e* before adding the suffix *-tion*. The plurals are irregular because of spelling changes from the singular form of the word. Some singular words ending in *o* have an *-es* added to make them plural, and others have only an *-s* added to make them plural.

Restudy the words in Review Words 506.

Spelling Words-2

Review Words 506

Suffix Words

addition	celebration	lonesome
afterward	fabulous	quarrelsome
authorship	friendship	relationship
burdensome	homeward	separation
cautious		

Irregular Plurals

beliefs	heroes	solos
echoes	pianos	thieves
halves		

Complete these activities.

2.90 Write the correct suffix word for each root word or word part.

a. add _____

b. celebrate _____

c. separate _____

d. caution _____

e. relation _____

f. lone _____

g. after _____

h. burden _____

i. fabul- _____

j. author _____
k. friend _____
l. quarrel _____
m. home _____

2.91   Write the irregular plurals for these singular words.
     a. half _____
     b. thief _____
     c. piano _____
     d. hero _____
     e. echo _____
     f. solo _____
     g. belief _____

Ask your teacher to give you a practice spelling test of Spelling Words-2. Restudy any words you miss.

Handwriting. Remember to watch the shape of your letters. Ovals and loops should be open and lines closed. The size of your letters should be uniform in both height and width.

Rewrite this sentence correctly using the proper shape and size of letters.

2.92

the proper shape and size of letters is important.

Review the material in this section to prepare for the Self Test. The Self Test will check your understanding of this section and will review the first section. Any items you miss in this test will show you what areas you need to restudy.

SELF TEST 2

Write *true* **or** *false* (each answer, 2 points).

2.01 _____ A novel covers a short period of time.

2.02 _____ Cadence is a rhythmical pattern that is not completely regular.

2.03 _____ A limerick is not a type of poetry.

2.04 _____ Personification is using repetition of sounds.

2.05 _____ Drama is a story written to be acted in front of an audience.

2.06 _____ The action of a story is the plot.

2.07 _____ A fact tells what a person "thinks" or "feels."

2.08 _____ Implied meaning is the idea an author suggests without saying it outright.

2.09 _____ Short stories have long character descriptions.

2.010 _____ We make Christian judgments when we decide what is right and wrong according to God's Word.

Match the following items (each answer, 2 points).

2.011 _____ asked to see if you
understand what you read

2.012 _____ the action is not long or involved

2.013 _____ what makes something happen

2.014 _____ a summary of all the
details in a reading selection

2.015 _____ phrases with meanings
that cannot be understood from the
ordinary meanings of the words in it

2.016 _____ helps you feel like being a
better person

2.017 _____ placing events in proper order

2.018 _____ has rhythm but not rhyme

2.019 _____ story poem that can be sung

2.020 _____ result or the outcome

a. main idea

b. sequence of events

c. comprehension questions

d. cause

e. effect

f. idioms

g. ballad

h. free verse

i. conundrums

j. inspirational poetry

k. short story

Choose the correct answer for each item. Write the letter and the answer on the lines (each answer, 2 points).

2.021   An author writes to entertain, to inform, to give facts, directions, or influence thinking. We call the author's reason for writing, the author's
_____ .

    a. purpose   b. authority   c. skill

2.022   An important reading comprehension skill is to identify the setting, characters, and _____ .

    a. life style   b. descriptions   c. plot

2.023   When you infer, or speculate, between events, you _____ .
    a. expect a surprise ending
    b. decide what probably happened
    c. make a Christian judgment

2.024   In the sentence, "Please *record* this title in the book and then play your new *record*," *record* is an example of _____ .
    a. implied meaning   b. idiom   c. heteronyms

2.025   "Fly like a bird," is an example of a _____ .
    a. pen picture   b. simile   c. imitation of sounds

2.026   When one thing stands for another, it is called _____ .
    a. symbolism   b. cadence   c. stanza

2.027   An exaggerated tale is called a _____ .
    a. fable   b. parable   c. legend

2.028   Poetry is written in _____ .
    a. stanzas   b. paragraphs   c. symbols

2.029   A short story that is meant to teach a lesson or moral is called a
_____ .

    a. metaphor   b. fable   c. legend

2.030   Diacritical marks and respellings show _____ .
    a. meanings   b. syllables and   c. idioms
                                   pronunciations

Read each past tense verb form. Write *R* if it is regular and *IR* if it is irregular (each answer, 1 point).

2.031   _____   bought

2.032   _____   prayed

2.033   _____   dropped

2.034   _____   broke

Select a verb from the list so the verbs and nouns agree in number (each answer, 1 point).

                          am were is are was

2.035   The tigers _____ in a cage.

2.036   The child _____ lonely.

Write the possessive form for each word (each answer, 1 point).

2.037   teacher _____

2.038   schools _____

Write the word from each sentence that matches its description (each answer, 2 points).

        The young man ran very quickly.

2.039   verb _____

2.040   adverb _____

2.041   adjective _____

2.042   adverb modifying an adverb _____

        George is going home.

2.043   common noun _____

2.044   proper noun _____

2.045   helping verb _____

2.046   participle _____

        She never saw a radiantly beautiful sunset.

2.047   adverb modifying an adjective _____

2.048   pronoun _____

2.049   negative adverb _____

        The cat wagged its tail, but the dog wagged its tail faster.

2.050   possessive pronoun _____

2.051   adverb showing comparison _____

        The raging river overflowed.

2.052   participle used as an adjective modifier _____

Complete this activity (each answer, 2 points).

2.053 What are the three verb tenses? _____

2.054 Write a sentence giving an example of one of the tenses. _____

_____

Possible Score   100

My Score   _____

Teacher check   _____

                     Initial   Date

 **Take a spelling test of Spelling Words-2.**

III. SECTION THREE

In this section you will review reading and Bible-study skills, kinds and uses of sentences, and you will write a dialogue and a personal reaction. You will restudy selected spelling words from Language Arts LIFEPAC 507, 508, and 509. In handwriting, you will practice two more handwriting tips.

SECTION OBJECTIVES

Review these objectives. When you have finished this section, you should be able to:

22. Identify information and details by scanning, skimming, and reading slowly.
23. Identify graphic aids and their uses.
24. Summarize.
25. Compare and contrast characters.
26. Use reading skills in Bible study.
27. Identify four kinds of sentences and punctuate them correctly.
28. Identify complete sentences, subject and predicate parts.
29. Arrange words in correct order.
30. Improve sentences by adding adjectives, adverbs, and using words correctly.
31. Write dialogue.
32. Spell words correctly.

Restudy these vocabulary words.

dialogue   graphic   summarize

USING READING AND BIBLE-STUDY SKILLS

You will review scanning, skimming, and reading slowly for details. You will also review how to use **graphic** aids, outlining, summarizing, comparing and contrasting, and two ways to use reading in your Bible study.

Scanning, skimming, and reading slowly for details. *Scanning* is a skill good readers use to find out if the material is what they want or need to read. When you scan, you do not read all the material. You only read enough here and there to give you an idea of what the material is about. *Skimming* is a similar skill to scanning. You also *do not* read all the material. You have in your mind what information you want to look for and then skim the materials looking for that specific information. Reading *slowly for details* simply means that if you need to remember the details of the material you are reading, read slowly enough to retain the information.

Complete these activities.

3.1   Scan the paragraph that follows 3.2. Circle the general subject or content of the material.
       scientific material   personal experience   mythical story

3.2   Skim the following paragraph to find where Beowulf lived. Write the answer.
       He lived in _____ .

Grendel, a mythical monster that was half man and half beast, stalked about killing the good people of Denmark. Beowulf was living in Sweden when he heard about the terrible terror his Danish friends were experiencing. He took fourteen men and went to King Hrothgar to volunteer his service. He would conquer Grendel once and for all! The king accepted Beowulf's offer. After a great feast, Beowulf and his companions lay down in the hall to await Grendel's coming.

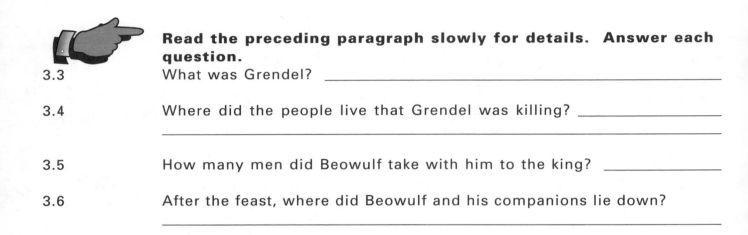

Read the preceding paragraph slowly for details. Answer each question.

3.3   What was Grendel? _____

3.4   Where did the people live that Grendel was killing? _____
_____

3.5   How many men did Beowulf take with him to the king? _____

3.6   After the feast, where did Beowulf and his companions lie down?
_____

Using graphic aids. You have learned how to get information from graphic aids such as maps, charts, diagrams, captions, illustrations, and time lines. A *map* helps you visualize where places are located and what is described. A *chart* displays information in a table or graph so you can get information easily. *Diagrams* describe, show size, show how something is used, how it works, or is put together. A diagram can show things in relation to other things. *Captions* are short explanations above or under an illustration to help you understand the illustration. *Illustrations* can tell you about the character or characters in a story, the action of a story, the setting, or even the content of the reading material. Illustrations can identify a problem. *A time line* shows you events in the order in which they have occurred. A time line gives you a quick and useful picture of major events.

 **Match these items.** Decide which graphic aid would best illustrate each item.

3.7 _____ to display the books of the New
Testament in four basic categories

3.8 _____ to picture major historical events
such as creation, man's fall, flood,
and so forth

3.9 _____ to picture the continent of Africa

3.10 _____ to picture how to assemble a model
airplane

3.11 _____ to picture a boy lost in the woods

3.12 _____ to explain the shapes of the
illustrated forms of galaxies

a. map
b. chart
c. diagram
d. caption
e. illustration
f. time line

Outlining. Outlining is another skill that will increase your reading comprehension. When you organize the important facts of a story into an outline, it helps you remember what you have read.

In Language Arts LIFEPAC 508, you were asked to read the parable "The Lost Son" in Luke 15:11–32. Reread this passage and then follow the directions for completing an outline.

 Complete the following outline on "The Lost Son" in Luke 15:11–22. Select topics and subtopics from the following list.

The departure
Father orders best robe, ring, and shoes for son
Son is sorry for sins
The repentance
Famine comes to the land
Father gives inheritance to son
Father runs and kisses son

3.13

I. _____
    A. Son asks for inheritance
    B. _____
    C. Son goes to far country
    D. Son wastes inheritance

II. The Misery of the Far Country
    A. _____
    B. Sons feeds swine
    C. Son eats with swine

III. _____
    A. Son remembers father's servants
    B. Son decides to return home
    C. _____
IV. The Return
    A. _____
    B. Son tells of his unworthiness
    C. _____

Summarizing. To **summarize** is to tell the main ideas or actions of a story as briefly as possible. Since an outline organizes the important facts of a story or an article, it can be helpful when writing a summary.

Summarize the parable, "The Lost Son" in Luke 15:11–22. Use the outline you just finished.

3.14   Luke 15:11–22: _____

_____

_____

_____

_____

_____

_____

_____

_____

_____

Teacher check _____
                      Initial   Date

Comparing and contrasting. When you *compare*, you look at the likeness between two or more things or people. When you *contrast,* you look at the differences. In LIFEPAC 504, you learned to compare and contrast the people in a story or someone from a story with someone from another story.

Read these character descriptions of *Mafatu*, the main character in *Call It Courage* (LIFEPAC 502), and *Esther* from "Esther" (LIFEPAC 509). As you read, think about their likenesses and differences.

Mafatu was called the "Boy Who Was Afraid." The early Polynesians worshiped courage. Mafatu was the son of the Great Chief of Hikueru. He was always afraid, so the people drove him away by indifference. Finally, Mafatu went out to face the thing he feared most, the sea. The people of Hikueru still sing his story in their chants.

Esther was a Jewish woman chosen by King Ahasuerus to be his new queen. Esther's cousin, Mordecai, asked her to go before the king to save her people from destruction. Esther knew that the king put to death anyone not called by the king. At first she was frightened, but she did appear before the king uncalled. This courageous woman was willing to place her life in God's hands to do His will.

Complete these activities.

3.15   Write one or two sentences describing the differences between Mafatu and Esther. _____
_____
_____
_____
_____
_____
_____

3.16   Write one or more sentences describing the similarities between Mafatu and Esther. _____
_____
_____
_____

Studying the Bible. God tells us in 1 Peter 2:2, "As newborn babes, desire the sincere milk of the word, that ye may grow thereby;" God wants us to desire His Word that we may as Peter says (2 Peter 3:18), "...grow in grace, and in knowledge of our Lord and Saviour Jesus Christ...." God wants to produce Christlike characteristics in us. As Christians we need to study God's Word and depend on His direction through the Holy Spirit in our lives.

In Language Arts LIFEPAC 509 you learned to use the reading skills of scanning, skimming, and reading slowly for details in your Bible study. In Language Arts LIFEPAC 502 you learned to use a chart, a graphic aid, to organize information from a Bible passage to help you remember the passage.

Complete these activities.

3.17   Scan the verses that follow 3.18. Circle the general subject or content of the verses.

proverbs of warning   trusting in the Lord   Bible history

3.18   Skim the following verses to find three commands that begin each verse. Write the three words. _____

Psalm 37:3–5

3. Trust in the Lord, and do good; so shalt thou dwell in the land, and verily thou shalt be fed.
4. Delight thyself also in the Lord; and he shall give thee the desires of thine heart.
5. Commit thy way unto the Lord; trust also in him; and he shall bring it to pass.

Read the preceding verses slowly for details. Answer each question.

3.19   Verse three states that God wants you to trust in Him and do what? _____

3.20   If you delight yourself in the Lord, what will he give you? _____
_____

3.21   What does the Lord ask you to commit to Him? _____

Complete this chart. Use the verses in Psalm 37:3–5.

3.22

God wants me to		If I obey God, He will	
1.	Trust in Him and do good	1.	_____ _____
2.	Delight in Him	2	_____ _____
3.	Commit my way to Him and trust in Him	3.	_____ _____

Write one thing that most impressed you in these verses.

3.23   I was most impressed with _____

_____

RECOGNIZING AND WRITING SENTENCES

You will review the four kinds of sentences and how to punctuate them correctly. You will also review complete sentences, sentence parts, and sentence order. You will review writing better sentences.

As you complete this section, you will also find out what happened to King Milford and his squire.

After trudging through Dragon Forest, King Milford found a note pinned to a tree. Help the king find out what the message says. The clues are circled and numbered in this section.

Kinds of sentences and punctuation. Review the four kinds of sentences and each example.

1.   Statement: I live in Arizona.
2.   Command or polite request:
     Bring me a piece of paper. (command)
     Please shut the door. (polite request)
3.   Question: Where are you going?
4.   Exclamation: Look at that fire!

Complete this activity.

3.24   Read these sentences and punctuate them with a period (.), a question mark(?), or an exclamation point (!). On the line after each sentence, write what kind of sentence it is: statement, request or command, question, or exclamation.

a. Please come inside _____   _____

b. Do you have change for a quarter _____   _____

c. Help, I'm sinking _____   _____

d. Go to the door _____   _____

e. Terry plays a trumpet _____   _____

Complete sentences, sentence parts, and sentence order. A complete sentence has two main parts: subject and predicate. A sentence expresses a complete thought. The subject part tells *who* or *what* the sentence is about. The predicate part tells what the subject *is, did, does,* or *was.*

Complete Sentence

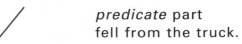

subject part   *predicate* part
A large box   fell from the truck.

Identify the complete sentences. Write <u>CS</u> on the line if the words produce a complete thought.

3.25   _____   The tortoise crawled across the desert sand.
3.26   _____   Raised a new variety of tomatoes.
3.27   _____   The cowboys rounded up the cattle.
3.28   _____   The sailboat drifted on the lake.
3.29   _____   A film about Canada.

Write *S* if the word group is a subject part and write *P* if the word group is a predicate part.

3.30   _____   Ate his dinner quickly.

3.31   _____   Carefully counted each item.

3.32   _____   The hot-air balloon.

3.33   _____   Played a new song on the piano.

3.34   _____   The angry pitcher.

The arrangement of words in a certain way is necessary to create sentences. The correct arrangement of words is called sentence order. Read these words.

> Bear the climbed tree a.

The preceding group of words is sufficient to make a complete sentence, but the group of words is not a sentence.

The words need to be rearranged into a meaningful order. Read the words in this box. They express a complete thought in the correct order.

> The bear climbed a tree.

In Language Arts LIFEPAC 505, you learned that putting words or phrases in a wrong place can make a very strange sentence.

> A boy planted a garden *in my* class.

The modifying phrase, *in my class*, is in the wrong place. It modifies or tells about the boy. Read the sentence with the correct word order.

> A boy in my class planted a garden.

 Rewrite these sentences putting the words in a proper order.

3.35   Rode bicycle John his the store to.
_____

3.36   The girl bought a plant with a hat.
_____

3.37   Bird a nesting is the tree in.
_____

3.38   The lion befriended the man with a hurt paw.
_____

Better written sentences. You can improve sentences by adding adjectives and adverbs, using proper word order, and choosing the correct words.

In Language Arts LIFEPAC 505 you also learned the right and wrong usage of certain words.

Example: Wrong - Leave me do it.
Right - Let me do it.

 **Complete these activities.**

3.39 Improve this sentence by adding adjectives.
The puppet sat on the dresser.

_____

3.40 Improve this sentence by adding adverbs.
The little child sat in his yard.

_____

3.41 Choose the right word. Write it on the line.

My mother _____ me how to sew at home.
taught   learned

③

Did you solve the mystery of King Milford's squire?

WRITING DIALOGUE AND A PERSONAL REACTION

In this composition section you will write the last two selections for your folder: a **dialogue** and a personal reaction.

Dialogue. In Language Arts LIFEPAC 505, you learned how to write and punctuate dialogue. Good dialogue can carry a story along and help the reader understand the characters. You learned that what the characters say must sound natural. A two-year old will not talk like a ten-year old. The way dialogue is written is called "direct quotation" because it quotes directly the exact words of the speaker. Dialogue requires a few special rules of punctuation to show which words are the words of each speaker. Review these rules of punctuation for dialogue.

1. The words of the speaker must be inside quotation marks (" ").

Examples: "Come home now," Bob said.
Bob called, "Come home now."

2. The words of the speaker must be separated from the words that tell who is speaking.

   a. Use a question mark (?) after the speaker's words if the speaker's words ask a question.

Example: "Who is there?" asked Linda.

   b. Use an exclamation mark (!) after the words of the speaker if the words show strong feeling.

Example: "What a mean thing to do!" exclaimed Terry.

   c. In all other direct quotations, separate the speaker's words from the rest of the sentence with a comma.

Example: "I am going to my room now," said Tim.

                (Notice that the comma is after the speaker's words.)

Example: Tim said, "I am going to my room."

                (Notice that the comma is after the words that tell who was speaking.)

3. The first words of the direct quotation must be capitalized.
4. Each time a different person speaks, start a new paragraph.

Example: "What made you so late?" his mother called from the kitchen. "Where are you, anyway?"
                "Here, washing my hands," Roger answered.

Complete this activity.

3.42   On a separate piece of paper, write a dialogue between two people. Be sure to write it the way those people would talk. Write the dialogue with correct punctuation. Your dialogue should be two or more paragraphs in length. You may choose one of the following ideas or one of your own. Place the dialogue in your composition folder.

Ideas for a Dialogue
A ten-year-old telling a story to an interrupting two-year old
Two friends talking about a game
A father discussing the stars with his son

Teacher check _____

                Initial   Date

A personal reaction. In Language Arts LIFEPAC 507, you read about Gulliver's personal reaction to the little people of Lilliput. A reaction is a response to a situation, a person, or a place. When writing a reaction, you will need to use reaction words. Review this list of reaction words.

happy	startled	frightened	proud
pleased	concerned	shy	amazement
excited	envied	embarrassment	nervous
sad	sympathy	disgust	disappointment
scared	anger	enthusiasm	

Read this example of a short personal reaction. The reaction words are in italics.

> **Example:** I was *excited* on the first day at my new school. However, I was *too shy* and *nervous* to talk to anyone.

Complete this activity.

3.43   On a separate piece of paper, write a personal reaction one or two paragraphs in length. You may choose one of the following ideas or one of your own. Place your personal reaction in the composition folder.

Ideas for a personal reaction
A trip you have taken	A new situation
An embarrassing moment	An unhappy moment
A person you met	An exciting time

Teacher check _____

                Initial   Date

SPELLING AND HANDWRITING

In this section you will review twenty words from each of the Language Arts LIFEPACs 507, 508, and 509. You will also review two more handwriting tips: stroke and slant.

Spelling. In Language Arts LIFEPAC 507, you learned how to spell homonyms, words with the /sh/ and the /aw/ sounds, words spelled with -ough, -aught, and -ought, and sight words.

Homonyms are words that are pronounced the same but have different meanings and spellings. The /sh/ sound can be spelled with a -ch, -s, -ss, -tion, or -sion. The /aw/ sound is found in words spelled with -aught, -ought, -augh, and -ough, but these words also have other sounds. Be careful! Watch out for sight words. They have irregular spellings.

Restudy the words from Spelling Word-3, Review Words 507.

Spelling Words-3

Review Words 507

Homonyms

cite	idle	minor
sight	idol	miner

/sh/ Spellings

chef	insure	vicious
emotion	mission	vision

/aw/ Sound, -aught, -ought, Sight Words

brief	drought	shriek
caught	fought	tough
conquer	rhythm	

Complete these activities.

3.44   Complete each sentence with the correct homonym word.

a.   She will _____ the Bible passage that tells how Paul

lost his _____ on the Damascus Road.

b.   The tribe was not _____ in the work of building a

new _____ to worship.

67

c. The _____ did not know the boy was a
_____ when he hired him to work in the mine.

3.45   Fill in the correct letters to complete the /sh/ sound in each word.

a. _____ ef   c. vi_____   e. mi _____ ion

b. vi_____   d. emo_____   f. in _____ ure

3.46   Write the two words with the /aw/ sound.

a. _____   b. _____

3.47   Complete these sentences with -ough and -ought words, and sight words.

a. John heard an eerie _____ come from the house.

b. It was _____ for the natives to survive the _____ during harvest season.

c. He liked the distinct _____ of the poem.

d. Sarah left for a _____ vacation.

e. The king tried to _____ the known world.

In Language Arts LIFEPAC 508 you learned to spell words with -ure, -age, -ion, -al, -ial, -ual and more homonyms.

Restudy the words in Review Words 508.

Spelling Words-3

Review Words 508

Suffix Words

burial	literature	rapture
comical	marriage	Scripture
conclusion	measure	spiritual
editorial	musical	supervision
eventual	procedure	usage
failure		

Homonyms

waist	way
waste	weigh

3.48   Complete these sentences with the correct homonym words.
    a. Would you please _____ yourself on this scale before you
       proceed on your _____ home?
    b. He ate all the food because he did not want to _____ it,
       but he knew his own _____ would suffer for it.

In Language Arts LIFEPAC 509 you learned to spell words with several syllables, sight words, and homonyms with a long *e*. The words with several syllables included (1) compound words that are divided between two words, (2) words with double consonants that are divided between the consonants, and (3) words beginning with *a* that are divided after the *a* when it is next to a single consonant, and are divided between the double consonants when the *a* is next to the double consonants (examples: about, allow).

You will review some sight words with silent letters, different spellings of the /l/ sound and the *s* as a /z/ sound.

Restudy the words in Review Words 509.

Spelling Words-3

Review Words 509

Syllables

abandon	apparent	rascal
account	fireplace	teammate
adopt	puppet	

Sight Words

alley	delight	fatal
bottle	exercise	nickel

Homonyms

feat	piece	steal
feet	peace	steel

Complete these activities.

3.49   Fill in the missing syllable.
        a. pup_____   c. ras_____   e. _____parent   g. team____
        b. a_____   d. a_____don   f. ac_____   h. fire_____

3.50   Write the three sight words with a spelling of the /l/ sound.
        a. _____   b. _____   c. _____

3.51   Fill in the letter or letters that may cause incorrect spelling in these
        sight words.
        a. all ___ y   b. exerci___ e   c. deli ___ t

3.52   Complete each sentence with the correct homonym word.
        a. The circus trapeze artist's greatest _____ was to hang from
           the trapeze by his _____ .
        b. The country asked for a declaration of _____ before the
           enemy decided to take a larger _____ of their land.
        c. People who _____ usually end up behind _____
           bars.

**Ask your teacher to give you a practice spelling test of
Spelling Words-3.** Restudy any words you miss.

Handwriting. Practice the last two tips for good handwriting:
stroke and slant. Stroke means the correct curved or straight
beginnings and endings of letters and the correct upward or downward
movement. Holding your paper diagonally will help you make slanted
strokes.

Complete this activity.

3.53   Rewrite this sentence correctly using the proper strokes and slant.

Use the proper strokes and slant.

Before you take this last Self Test, you may want to do one or more of these self checks.

1. _____ Read the objectives. See if you can do them.
2. _____ Restudy the material related to any objectives that you cannot do.
3. _____ Use the SQ3R study procedure to review the material.
    a. **S**can the sections.
    b. **Q**uestion yourself.
    c. **R**ead to answer your questions.
    d. **R**ecite the answers to yourself.
    e. **R**eview areas you did not understand.
4. _____ Review all vocabulary words, activities, and Self Tests, writing a correct answer for every wrong answer.

SELF TEST 3

Write *true* **or** *false* (each answer, 2 points).

3.01 _____ Maps help you visualize where places are located.

3.02 _____ When you compare and contrast, you just tell the differences.

3.03 _____ You can use reading skills to study the Bible.

3.04 _____ Dialogue requires special rules of punctuation.

3.05 _____ A simile has imitation of sounds.

3.06 _____ A novel is a short story.

3.07 _____ The "main idea" is a summary of all the details in a reading selection.

3.08 _____ Inspirational poetry makes you feel like being a better person.

3.09 _____ Metaphor is the rhythmical pattern of a poem.

3.010 _____ Idioms can be understood from the ordinary meaning of the words.

Match the following items (each answer, 2 points).

3.011 _____ short explanation of a drawing		a. scan
3.012 _____ one thing standing for another		b. skim
3.013 _____ type of poetry		c. read slowly
3.014 _____ decide what probably happened		d. caption
3.015 _____ to remember details		e. symbolism
3.016 _____ words having different meanings		f. short stories
and pronunciations, but spelled		g. novel
the same		h. rhymed quatrain
3.017 _____ to look for specific details		i. cadence
3.018 _____ have brief character descriptions		j. speculate between events
3.019 _____ a rhythmical pattern that is not		k. heteronym
completely regular		
3.020 _____ to find general content		

Choose the correct answer for each item. Write the letter and answer on the blank (each answer, 2 points).

3.021   A skill that helps you organize the important facts of a passage is called

_____ .

      a. illustrating   b. outlining   c. scanning

3.022   A map, a chart, and a diagram are examples of _____ .

      a. graphic aids   b. time lines   c. captions

3.023   When you tell the main ideas or actions of a story as briefly as possible, it is called _____ .

      a. summarizing   b. outlining   c. skimming

3.024   A complete sentence must have a subject part and a(n)

_____ .

      a. adjective   b. adverb   c. predicate part

3.025   A response to a situation, a person, or a place is called a

_____ .

      a. dialogue   b. reaction   c. usage

3.026   A story written to be acted in front of an audience is _____ .

      a. a fable   b. a novel   c. drama

3.027   When we decide what is right and wrong according to God's Word, we make _____ .

      a. fables   b. Christian judgments   c. morals

3.028   When an author suggests a meaning without saying it outright, it is called _____ .

      a. implied meaning   b. stationary meaning   c. plot

3.029   A story poem that can be sung is called _____ .

      a. a short poem   b. lyrical   c. a ballad

3.030   When an author tells what he "feels" or "thinks," he is stating his

_____ .

      a. descriptions   b. fact   c. opinion

Write the word from each sentence that matches its description (each answer, 2 points).

A sleeping John lay quietly on the soft bed.

3.031   verb _____

3.032   adverb _____

3.033   participle used as an adjective modifier _____

3.034   common noun _____

3.035   proper noun _____

3.036   adjective _____

The wet beaver is shaking its tail.

3.037   helping verb _____

3.038   possessive pronoun _____

Punctuate these sentences correctly (each answer, 2 points).

3.039   Who is going _____

3.040   Please close the door _____

3.041   An elephant is in your house _____

Write CS on the blank if the item is a sentence and N if it is not a sentence (each answer, 2 points).

3.042 _____ The couch was on sale.

3.043 _____ The new baseball equipment.

3.044 _____ The suitcase contained important papers.

3.045 _____ Looked at me strangely.

Underline the subject and circle the predicate part of this sentence (this answer, 2 points).

3.046   The healed man leaped for joy.

Punctuate this dialogue correctly (each punctuation mark, 1 point—total of 8 possible).

3.047   I'm going to the store now Mother said Bob replied May I go with you

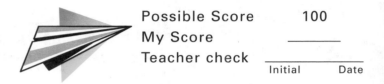

Possible Score   100
My Score   _____
Teacher check   _____
                              Initial   Date

   **Take a spelling test of Spelling Words-3.**

          Before taking the LIFEPAC Test, you may want to do one or more of these self checks.

1. _____   Read the objectives. See if you can do them.
2. _____   Restudy the material related to any objectives that you cannot do.
3. _____   Use the SQ3R study procedure to review the material.
4. _____   Review activities, Self Tests, and LIFEPAC vocabulary words.
5. _____   Restudy areas of weakness indicated by the last Self Test.